BIBLE STORIES & ACTIVITIES FOR CHILDREN

ANNE-MARIA BANKAY & DOREEN ELLIS
Illustrated by Haley Jones

Arawak publications Resource Publications
Kingston • Jamaica Eugene • Oregon

© 2022 by Anne-Maria Bankay & Doreen Ellis
All rights reserved. Published 2022

This edition licensed by special permission
from Arawak publications

ISBN 978-1-6667-3804-9 (paperback)
ISBN 978-1-6667-9824-1 (hardcover)
ISBN 978-1-6667-9825-8 (eBook)

Illustrations by Haley Jones

Photographs by Kamal W. Bankay and Merrick Cousley

Book design by Annika Lewinson-Morgan

Set in Calibri and OzHandicraft BT

CONTENTS

Dedication — 5

Preface — 6

Acknowledgements — 6

The Little Shepherd Boy Who Killed the Giant — 7

🧩 Join the Dots — 12

A Kind Boy's Lunch Feeds 5,000 People — 13

🧩 The Maze — 18

The Man God Used to Free His People — 19

🧩 Find the Secret Message! — 25

From Canaan to Egypt — 26

🧩 Word Search — 31

Love and Loyalty: Ruth and Naomi — 32

🧩 Spot the Differences! — 37

The Resurrection — 38

🧩 Crack the Code! — 43

God's Gift of Strength — 44

🧩 Join the Dots — 49

He Turned Water into Wine — 50

🧩 Crossword Puzzle — 54

Answers to Activities — 55

My Drawings — 58

LIST OF ILLUSTRATIONS FOR COLOURING

Young David tending the sheep and protecting them from harm — 8
David knocks Goliath out with a slingshot — 11
Jesus speaking to the crowd of people — 14
A little boy offers his lunch which fed 5,000 people — 16
The Hebrew people enslaved by the Egyptians — 20
Baby Moses in a basket near the river — 22
Joseph in his coat of many colours talking to his father, Jacob — 27
Joseph's brothers sell him as a slave — 30
Ruth and Naomi on the road to Bethlehem — 33
Ruth picking barley when Boaz comes by — 35
Mary at the tomb of Jesus — 39
The disciples hurry to the tomb of Jesus after His resurrection — 42
Samson kills a lion — 45
Samson destroys the Philistine temple — 48
Mary tells Jesus the wine is finished — 51
Jesus turns water into wine — 53

DEDICATION

This book is dedicated to my granddaughter,
Isla Rachel Bankay,
who was the inspiration for this book,
in the hope that it will contribute to her Christian life
and that of other children.

—*Anne-Maria Bankay*

This book is dedicated to my grandsons
Zachary and Xavier Ellis,
also Dominic Watson, my grandnephew,
who attempted his first illustration
and eventually led us to Haley.

—*Doreen Ellis*

PREFACE

The idea for this book came about while we were doing adult Bible Study. It occurred to us that we could make some of the stories we know, more accessible to young children who are in the age range of some of our grandchildren.

As we wrote the stories, we decided that activities based on the stories would provide some fun for the children at the same time as help them to remember what they had heard or read themselves. So, all the illustrations are in black and white so that the children can colour them as they would like. We hope the activities provide the children with many hours of fun and that they will enjoy the stories and want to return to them again and again.

ACKNOWLEDGEMENTS

We wish to express our sincere appreciation to the following people, who directly or indirectly helped to make this book a reality:

- » Haley Jones, our illustrator
- » Our reviewers – Mondrell Oz and Dr. Yewande Lewis-Fokum
- » Photographers, Kamal W. Bankay and Merrick Cousley
- » Publisher, Pansy Benn of Arawak publications
- » Book designer, Annika Lewinson-Morgan
- » Family members and friends who encouraged us.

The Little Shepherd Boy Who Killed the Giant

David was a shepherd. He looked after his father's sheep. Sometimes children help to look after their parents' goats, chickens, or even pet fish.

David was very brave. The sheep were in a big open field where animals like lions and bears roamed around. Sometimes these lions and bears would try to steal a sheep and David would use his stick to chase them away.

One day David's father said to him, "Today I want you to take some food to your brothers who are fighting in King Saul's army. They are fighting against some very strong men. The biggest and strongest is Goliath. The soldiers are afraid of him."

David hurried away to take the food to his brothers. He got there just when Goliath came out to boast. He was HUGE!

He said in a very loud, booming voice, "Which of you silly little soldiers can fight me? If I kill you, all your people will be our servants. But if you kill me, we will be your servants."

When King Saul's soldiers saw Goliath, they trembled and ran and hid themselves. They were so afraid.

But David said, "I'm not afraid of him, I will fight him. I have chased away lions and bears when they came to steal my sheep."

King Saul put some heavy clothes on David to protect him against the huge giant.

The clothes were too heavy for David to walk in, so he took them off.

David got five small stones from the nearby river and called out to Goliath. "I want to fight you."

Goliath laughed. "Ha ha ha. You silly little boy, you come to fight me, Goliath, with a sling shot and stones? I am going to kill you so fast."

But David said, "I come to you in the name of the Lord and today God is going to let me kill you."

He put one stone in his sling shot and aimed it at Goliath's head. *Woosh!*

A Kind Boy's Lunch Feeds 5,000 People

Jesus loved people and people loved him because he was always kind to them. He also healed people who were sick. Because of this, large crowds were always following him.

They also liked to listen to interesting stories Jesus told about God and about how we should treat other people even when they do not look like us.

Jesus had twelve very close friends. He called them Disciples. He taught them many lessons that would come in very handy when he left them.

One day, Jesus felt that his disciples were tired and needed some rest.

He told them, "Let's get away from these crowds for a while. We will use the boat and go over to the other side of the land so you can get some rest."

The crowds of people saw that Jesus and his disciples were leaving in the boat. They knew Jesus was going over to the other side. They ran and got there before the boat. When Jesus and his disciples reached, there was already a crowd.

Although Jesus and his disciples were tired, he still healed sick people who were brought to him and he still told the people interesting stories.

The people were now hungry and the disciples told Jesus, "Let us send them away so they can go and get food."

The little boy gave up his lunch.

Jesus blessed it, broke it up in small pieces and told the disciples to serve it to the people.

That small lunch fed over five thousand people. Everyone had a full belly and there were leftovers!

If we are willing,
God can use whatever we have,
no matter how small, to help others.

The Maze

Follow the numbers to find the way through the maze.

1	4	5	6	7
2	15	14	13	8
3	6	9	10	10
4	7	10	11	12
5	8	9		13
6	7	8	11	14
11	14	13	12	15
10	15	15	14	16
20	16	16		17
19	18	17		18
			20	19

See answer on page 55.

The Man God Used to Free His People

This is the story about a man whose name was... well, he did not have a name at the beginning. We are about to see how he got his name.

He lived in a country which had big seas and rivers and many fruit trees. This was really not his country, but his family moved there many, many years before he was born. The name of the country was Egypt.

The King of Egypt did not like the people who had come to live in Egypt. He made them do all of the hard work.

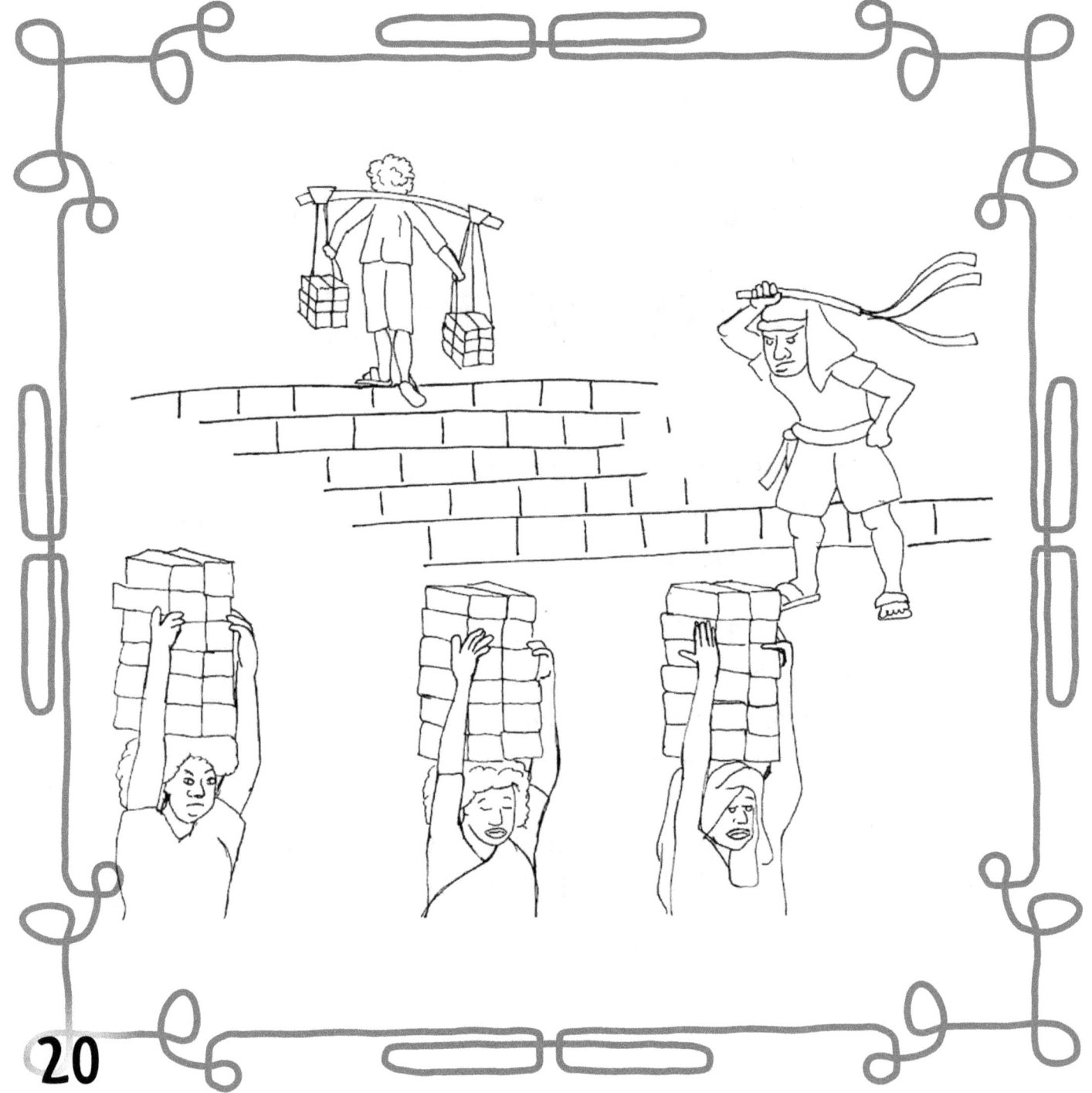

He was afraid. "What if they become too many and try to fight us. What shall I do?"

He scratched his head and thought, and thought. "I've got it!" he said. "The men are the ones who fight, so if I get rid of all boy babies there will be no men to fight us."

This was a very unkind plan.

One day a pretty little baby boy was born in this family. His mother said, "I cannot let them get my baby. I will hide him."

So she wrapped him carefully in a blanket. Then she put him in a little basket. She tip-toed quietly to the door of the house. As she opened it, she heard a rustle. She froze. Then she heard a flap, flap and a screech.

"Oh," she said to herself, "it's just a screech owl."

The next day the King's daughter said to her maids, "What a hot day! Come, let's go down to the river and splash around."

As they got close, they heard a sound coming from the bushes. It sounded like a kitten.

"What's that sound? Wonder if it's a kitten caught in the bushes?" she said.

As they got closer to the sound and looked, it was a baby! She was so excited, she decided to take the baby home.

"Let's call him Moses," she said, "because I pulled him up out of the river bushes. Now, I will need a nurse to care for him. Anybody knows of a good nurse?"

"I do," said Miriam, Moses' sister, who was hiding nearby, and she went and got Moses' mother.

So, Moses grew up in the King's house, cared for by his own mother.

When Moses grew up, God used him to free his family from Egypt.

God watches over us and can use us to do great things for him.

Find the Secret Message!

Cross out the word "MOSES" every time you see it.
Use the letters remaining to form a secret message.

MOSESGMOSESOMOSESDMOSESL
MOSESOMOSESVMOSESEMOSESS
MOSESUMOSESSMOSESVMOSESE
MOSESRMOSESYMOSESMMOSES
UMOSESCMOSESHMOSESMOSES

Secret Message:

_ _ _   _ _ _ _ _   _ _

_ _ _ _   _ _ _ _

See answer on page 55.

25

From Canaan to Egypt

One day after I had breakfast, my father, Jacob, said to me, "Joseph, go into the field and see how your brothers are doing. You know they are looking after the sheep."

I put on the beautiful coloured coat that my father had given me for a gift, and I walked to where my brothers were working.

My brothers were not happy to see me. They were upset because some days before, I told them about two dreams I had.

They said the dreams meant that I would rule over them and they did not like that. They were also unhappy because I was the only one who got a new coat.

The next thing I knew, I found myself in a deep, dark, hole. I felt alone and frightened. I believed I was going to die. I prayed to God to help me. I felt much better after that. I thought my brothers would come back for me and take me out of the hole, but none of them came.

The next morning they came, but they did not take me out of the hole. I heard voices above me, talking about money.

Afterwards some men I did not know gave my brothers twenty pieces of silver and they pulled me out of the hole. The men put me in the back of a cart and took me away.

After travelling for a long time, I was told that I was in Egypt. I was sold to a man named Potiphar to work in his house. I was a slave! No pay, just work.

I decided to work very hard and my master, Potiphar, was happy with me. I became the best worker in his household. Though I was away from my family and was now a slave, I was comfortable. I saw that God was taking care of me. I was not killed by the strange men and everything was going well for me in Potiphar's house at that time.

I gave God thanks every day.

Word Search

Search for the following 7 words from the story, From Canaan to Egypt, that are hidden in the puzzle below.

Joseph Jacob Egypt Canaan
Coat Silver Brothers

C	S	I	L	V	E	R	L	I	S
A	C	P	O	T	F	K	C	N	G
R	A	L	T	J	A	C	O	B	M
I	C	P	H	O	R	N	A	T	F
V	A	D	E	S	B	O	T	J	A
E	N	O	K	E	G	Y	P	T	M
R	A	J	O	P	H	W	E	L	M
S	A	T	M	H	R	D	Y	V	J
A	N	I	L	E	G	S	P	B	N
F	K	S	R	E	H	T	O	R	B

See answer on page 56.

Love and Loyalty: Ruth and Naomi

A young woman called Ruth was married to a man called Mahlon. They lived together in Moab with Mahlon's mother, Naomi.

When Mahlon died, Naomi had no more relatives there, because her husband and her other son had died before. She was sad and unhappy.

Naomi decided to return to Bethlehem, where she was born. She tried to get Ruth to return to her own family. Because Ruth was a Moabite she would not be welcomed easily by Naomi's people.

Ruth refused to leave Naomi. She promised her that she would follow her anywhere she was going and that she would never leave her and would even accept her God. Naomi was very happy because Ruth always took good care of her.

After a long journey, Ruth and Naomi arrived in Bethlehem. Everybody was surprised to see Naomi return. But there was a big problem. Naomi and Ruth were very poor. Not having a husband in those days meant that there was no money.

Ruth decided to go and work in the fields, picking barley. She worked very hard. One day Boaz, the rich owner of a field, saw Ruth and asked about her. He liked her and wanted to help her.

Even though Ruth was not one of his people, Boaz decided that he would marry her.

Ruth and Boaz lived happily together and they had a son who was named Jesse.

Jesse was the father of King David,
who was related to Jesus.

The Resurrection

It was Sunday – two days after Jesus had been crucified by Roman soldiers.

Jesus' friends were all sad. They did not expect him to die like that. He was so good and kind. How could the godly leaders not see that he was special? That he was the Son of God?

Jewish custom is to rub spices and oils on the body of a dead person before he or she is buried. This is called embalming. Mary, one of Jesus' friends, came very early to the tomb where Jesus was laid, to embalm his body. She was very sad.

When she arrived at the tomb, the huge, round stone that was used to block the opening of the tomb had been rolled away.

"Who could have done this?" she thought. She went to the opening and peeped in. "Oh my goodness!" Mary exclaimed. "His body is not here. Somebody must have stolen it."

"But why would anyone do such a thing?" she thought. She was even more sad than when she first came. She wanted so much to do this one last thing for her friend, Jesus, who had been so kind to her.

Mary turned away from the tomb puzzled. What should she do now?

As she walked away sadly, she saw a man nearby. It was Jesus, but she did not recognize him.

"This must be the gardener," she thought. "He might know what has happened to Jesus' body. I will ask him."

"Sir, do you have any idea who removed Jesus' body from the tomb? If you do, please tell me where they have taken him so I can go and embalm his body."

Jesus called her name. "Mary," he said, and immediately she recognized his voice and knew it was Jesus.

She was so happy. God had raised Jesus from the dead.

Jesus said to her, "Go and tell my friends that I am alive."

Jesus had told his disciples that he would be crucified but that on the third day God would raise him from the dead. His disciples did not understand, but now they did. They were all very happy.

Crack the Code!

Each of the letters has a secret code.
Use the secret code to fill the blanks below with
the right letter. Then say the word.

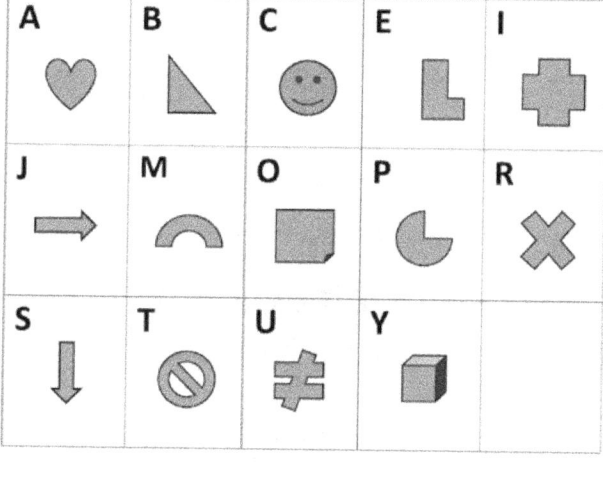

See answer on page 57.

God's Gift of Strength

Manoah and his wife did not have any children. They prayed to God for a child.

Manoah said to God, "Almighty Father, you know that we have waited many years for the gift of a child from you, but we are getting old and still we have no child."

God answered Manoah and told him, "I will bless you and your wife with a son, but on one condition. His hair should never be cut. Let his hair grow freely and never cut it."

So, Manoah and his wife had a son and named him Samson. They never cut his hair.

Samson was very, very strong and could do amazing things. One day he killed a lion with the jawbone of a dead donkey.

Samson became a leader of the Israelites and he was also a warrior.

Many people wanted to find out what made Samson so strong and tried to get him to tell them his secret. They would say, "Samson, tell us your secret. What makes you so strong?" But Samson never told them anything.

At that time, the Philistines were the enemies of the Israelites and were always trying to conquer them in battle. They realised that if they could capture Samson, the Israelites would not be able to win any more battles. So, they paid a woman named Delilah to get the secret out of Samson.

Every day she said to Samson, "Samson, if you love me, tell me what makes you so very strong."

At first, Samson did not tell her the secret but after a while he decided to tell her.

The secret of Samson's strength was his long hair and when Delilah heard that, she cut it off when Samson was sleeping. This made Samson weak and the Philistines were able to capture him. They removed his eyes and put him to work for them. Samson became a prisoner! But his hair started to grow back and as his hair grew, so did his strength.

One day, while the Philistines were enjoying themselves and having fun in a great temple, Samson asked some men to take him to a certain place where two columns were holding up the temple. Samson prayed to God to give him enough strength to destroy the temple and told God that he was prepared to die at the same time as the Philistines he wanted to kill.

Samson said to God, "Father in Heaven, I am asking you to give me enough strength to break down this temple when I shake the columns with my bare hands. Thousands of Philistines will die when the temple falls and I will die with them."

God gave Samson his wish and so Samson was able to destroy the temple and thousands of Philistines but he died with them.

Join the Dots

Complete the picture of the lion.

49

He Turned Water into Wine

Jesus and his disciples were invited to a wedding in a town called Cana. Suddenly one of the waiters who were serving realised that there was a big problem. He said, "Oh no! All the wine is finished and we still have guests to be served!"

Mary, Jesus' mother, was also at the wedding and she went to Jesus and said to him, "My son, the wine is finished and guests are still here, waiting to be served."

Jesus said to her, "Why are you telling me about the wine? That has nothing to do with me."

Jesus was really very surprised that his mother told him about the wine but he knew that she wanted him to help and to solve the problem.

Jesus' mother knew that her son would help because he was very kind. So, she told the people who were serving, "Do whatever Jesus tells you to do."

Jesus told them to fill six very large containers with water. Then Jesus told them to taste the water. Jesus had turned the water into wine! And it was the best wine they had ever tasted. It was a miracle! The first miracle that Jesus ever performed.

The people at the wedding were surprised but very happy, especially Jesus' mother because her son had performed his first miracle.

Crossword Puzzle

"He Changed Water to Wine"

Across:

2: What was put in the 6 jugs?

3: What important drink was finished?

4: What was the name of the town where the event was held?

Down:

1: Who performed the miracle?

2: What event was Jesus attending?

See answer on page 57.

Answers to Activities

Page 18 • The Maze

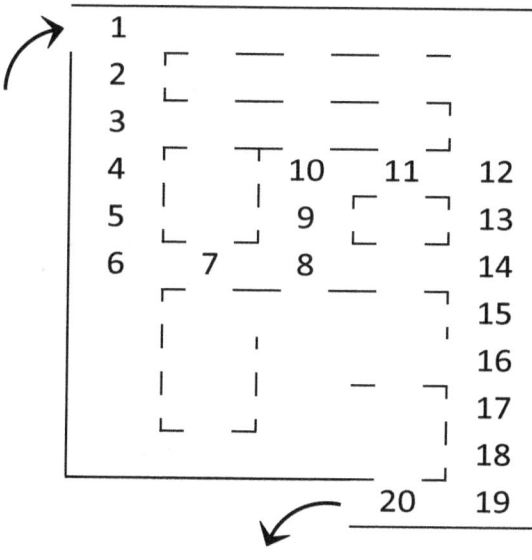

Page 25 • Find the Secret Message!

"God loves us very much."

Page 43 • Crack the Code!

Mary, Jesus, Tomb, Spice

Page 54 • Crossword Puzzle

My Drawings

www.ingramcontent.com/pod-product-compliance
Lightning Source LLC
Chambersburg PA
CBHW081637040426
42449CB00014B/3355